# EXTRAORDINARY RAIN FORESTS

## Contents

W9-BPN-088

# Hot House!

What is a rain forest? Easy — it's a forest where it rains a lot! But there's a lot more to it than that. Rain forests are home to a huge collection of the most extraordinary plants and animals on Earth. In fact, you can find more different kinds of life in just one square mile of rain forest than you would in a whole state!

## Where in the World?

Rain forests are found within a wide band on either side of the equator, which is an imaginary line around the Earth's middle. This band is called the tropics. In the rain forest, most of the rain falls during a wet season. A dry season then follows.

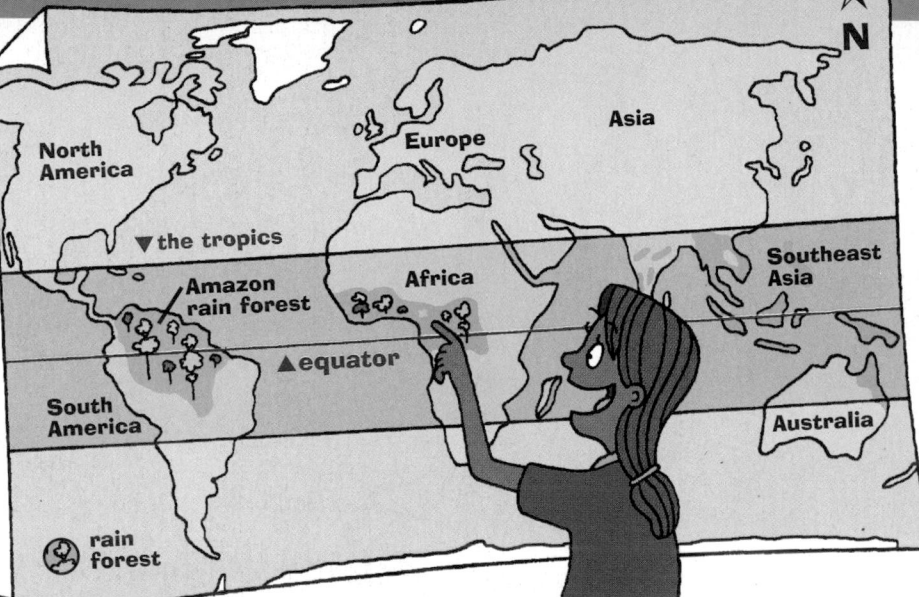

## Wild and Wet

Plants take in water from the ground. They give off unused water through their leaves, and this becomes rain. During a year, rain forests receive around 13 feet (4 m) of rain, enough to cover you four times over! More than half of this water comes from plants. How would you like to take a shower in tree sweat?

## Home Base

Each rain forest region has its own plants and animals that live there. For instance, the gorilla lives in Africa, while the spider monkey lives in South America. In Asia, you'll find the orangutan, while in Australia, you'll see the tree kangaroo. None of these animals will ever meet!

EXTRA! EXTRA!
This scene shows a rain forest in Borneo, Southeast Asia, jam-packed with trees. Like many other rain forests, it has a river snaking through it.

HA HA

A rain forest is dense, hot, wet, and steamy. Deep inside the forest's green darkness, trees and other plants fight for space and animals sing, squawk, howl, and scurry!

# What's the Story?

Think of the rain forest as a four-story apartment building, with different creatures living on each floor. So hop aboard the rain forest elevator for a tour. We'll start at the top, and go from the bright and sunny roof garden all the way down to the dark and dingy ground floor.

**EXTRA! EXTRA!**
An orangutan's arms are long enough to reach to its ankles. They're perfect for swinging through the trees!

▲ The orangutan is a red-haired ape that lives in the trees of Southeast Asian rain forests. Baby orangutans, such as these, stay with their mothers until they are eight years old.

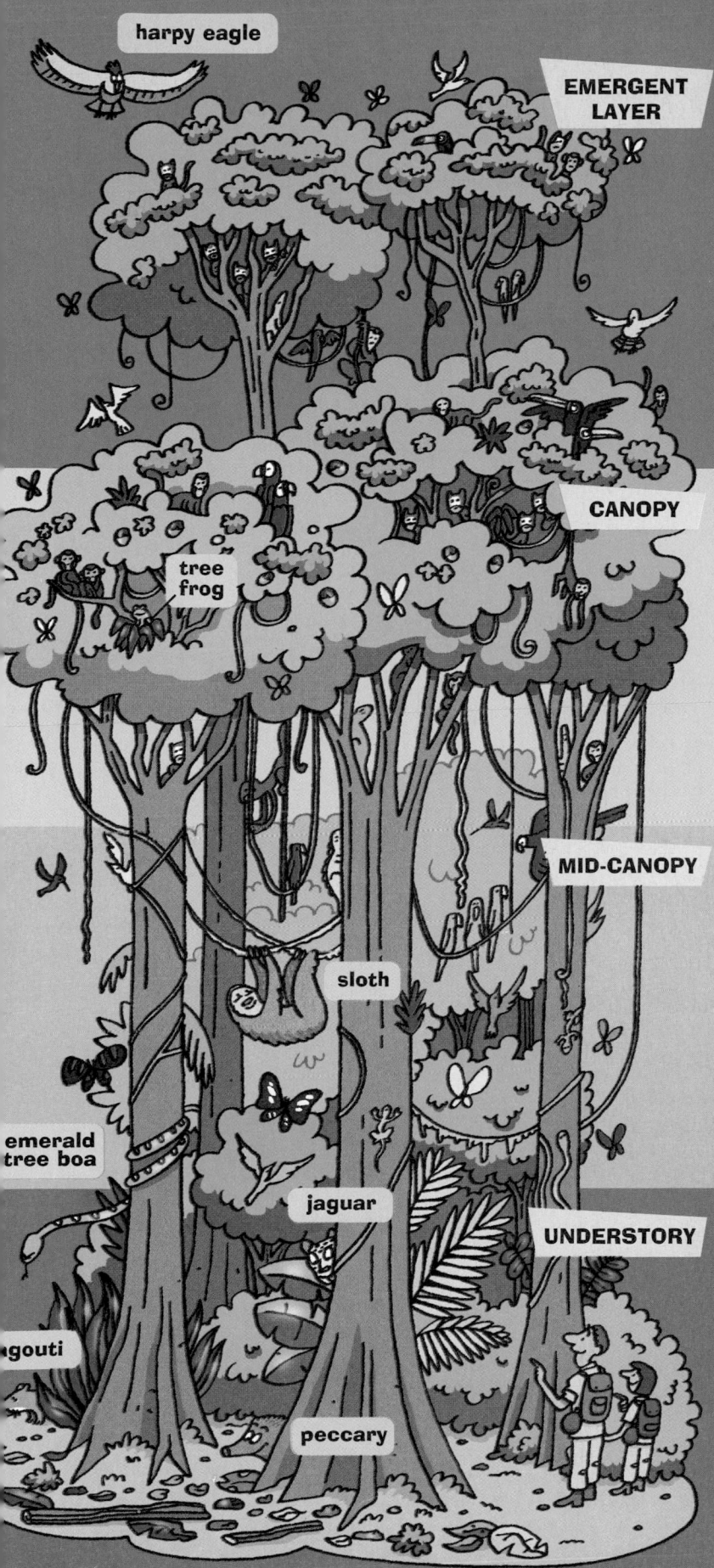

harpy eagle

**EMERGENT LAYER**

CANOPY

tree frog

MID-CANOPY

sloth

emerald tree boa

jaguar

UNDERSTORY

agouti

peccary

# Raising the Roof

The world's rain forests have similar features, but the one shown here is the Amazon rain forest in South America. At the top is the emergent layer, where trees poke their heads up above the others. Birds of prey nest here. These are birds, such as the harpy eagle, that attack other animals. They patrol the forest's rooftops for monkeys and birds.

# Green Room

Going down! The next layer is the leafy canopy, which is the busiest floor. It receives the most sun and rain, so lots of fruit and flowers grow here, supplying food for a huge variety of animals. Tree frogs lay eggs in the leaves of bromeliad plants. Butterflies and birds fly around.

# Shady Lane

Next stop is the mid-canopy. This zone is so full of branches, dangling roots, and vines that it's a perfect place for a sloth to hang out. The emerald tree boa snake slithers in the mid-canopy, unless he's just dropped down on a big, ratlike agouti for a quick meal!

# Down in the Dump

At the bottom is the understory, or the forest floor. The forest floor is covered in rotting leaves. Big mammals live here. Mammals are hairy animals, such as the jaguar, that feed their babies on mother's milk. Another mammal, the peccary, is a rain forest pig that slurps up any bugs, roots, and fallen fruit. Yum!

# Tree-mendous Talent!

Surviving in the treetops is a real challenge, but rain forest animals are well designed to cope with the high life. They have a full supply of tricks and features that help them to grasp, climb, swing, hover, and even make their homes far above the ground.

## That's Weird!

Geckos are small lizards with an incredible ability to cling onto a branch even when they are upside down. They have tiny scales on their toes that can sink into small cracks and get a grip on just about any surface.

I'm clinging in the rain!

## Hang On!

The monkeys of South America, such as this spider monkey, have a useful feature that their monkey cousins in Africa lack. They have strong, clinging tails that they use as a fifth hand for climbing through branches. The spider monkey also has super-long arms and legs for swinging from tree to tree.

# Home, Sweet Home

The tent-making bat has amazing homemaking skills! It bites through the main stem of a leaf, so that the leaf folds in half to make a tent shape. The holes the bat chews out then become grips for its toes, so it can spend its whole day hanging upside down. The tent protects the bat from sun, rain, and hunters. Up to 30 bats can share a tent.

Room in there for me?

## EXTRA! EXTRA!

The name *hummingbird* comes from the hum that the bird's wings make as it hovers. Its wings beat between 40 and 80 times a second!

The hummingbird is like a tiny helicopter. Its high-speed wing flaps help it to hover in one place and fly backward. It can even drink juice from a flower without landing.

# Power Plants

Life can be pretty tough for rain forest plants. Hungry animals want to eat them. Bigger plants, such as giant trees, hog up all the best sunshine and soak up the soil's richest plant food. In these conditions, rain forest plants have found crazy ways to survive!

## Go Large

Hardly any sunlight makes it to the forest floor, but the elephant-sized tree fern has a way to handle that problem. It grows massive leaves, called fronds, to make sure it catches the few rays that do make it through the thick canopy.

## Bug Soup

The pitcher plant likes to eat meat! It catches its prey by producing a sweet juice, called nectar, around its rim. When insects stop by for a drink, they fall into a liquid inside the plant. This turns them into bug soup — the plant's favorite meal. Small animals that try to steal the insects get souped up, too.

## Rain Forest Strangler

Almost there!

**1**

The strangler vine climbs trees to find sunlight. It takes nutrients from the soil to help it grow fast.

Gotcha!

**2**

Then the strangler vine covers the tree and steals the tree's light. The poor tree is done for!

The leaf of the Victoria amazonica water lily is one of the largest leaves in the world. Thick veins run along the bottom, which make it incredibly strong. If a small child sat on it, it would still float!

The Victoria amazonica is the largest water lily in the world. It grows in quiet, shallow rivers, where it is anchored to the muddy riverbed by a thick stem.

# Flower Forest

Q. WHAT DID THE FLOWER SAY TO THE BEE? A. YOU'VE BEE-N HERE BEFORE!

To make baby plants, flowers produce male cells in tiny grains called pollen. The pollen has to be spread around so that it can join with female cells in other plants. Flowers can't run around spreading pollen themselves, so they make animals do it for them. For this reason, many rain forest plants go all out to attract animals and get noticed!

HA HA

10

▲ The rafflesia is as big as a manhole cover. It copies the smell of rotten meat . . . which small flies love! They get covered with pollen when they come for a sniff.

# Bee-yootiful

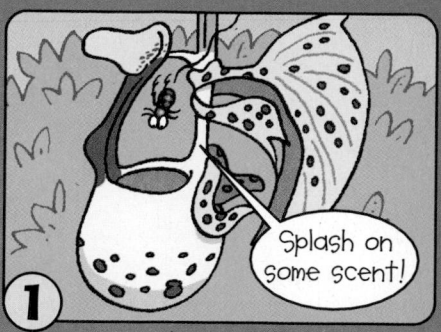

**Splash on some scent!**

**1** The sneaky bucket orchid plays a trick on male bees looking for a mate. The flower produces perfume that the bee spreads on himself to attract females.

**Yikes!**

**2** The bee scrapes the orchid's perfume off of the petals. But the flower is slippery and he falls into a bucket of liquid! Here you can see what happens inside the flower.

**Free at last!**

**3** Don't worry — there's an escape tunnel. As the male bee crawls through it, he is dusted with pollen. Now he flies off to spread pollen to other bucket orchids!

# Wow!

The flowering spike of the titan arum plant grows taller than an adult. It flowers only once every seven years. The flower lasts for only two days, so its smell has to be strong to attract insects quickly. It smells so bad to people that its nickname is the corpse flower!

**Ugh!**

## The Nose Knows

There are so many sights and smells in the rain forest that a greenish-yellow flower such as the ylang-ylang has to create something special to make animals come to it. It produces a scent so lovely that the oil from its flowers is made into one of the most expensive perfumes.

**Mmm... wish I could bottle that!**

## Crab That!

Colors and shapes get a flower noticed, too! These flowers, known as crab claws because of their odd shape, grow in the Amazon rain forest. Their bright red color helps them to attract hummingbirds. The collection of flowers shown here is nearly as tall as you are!

# Gentle Giants

Gorillas are some of the gentlest creatures on Earth. They spend their days roaming around the African rain forest searching for tasty plants to eat. They also like to snooze, play, and clean each other. They have only one natural enemy, which also happens to be one of their closest relatives: humans.

## Family Fun

Gorillas live together in a family, which contains between 5 and 30 members. The top gorilla in the group is an adult male. When a young male reaches the age of around 12, he leaves his family to start a new group. He bands together with young females or takes over the group of another male. As he grows older, he is called a silverback because the hairs on his back turn gray. The silverback is usually the father of all the group's babies.

## Camping Out

Just after sunrise, gorillas wake up. The group travels together during the day and makes a new camp each night. The gorillas make nests out of leaves and branches either on the ground or in the trees. Females sleep with their babies.

The gorilla looks fierce, but is naturally shy! There are fewer than 650 mountain gorillas left in the wild because their forest home is being cut down by people for wood and for farmland.

Q. WHAT DO YOU GET IF YOU CROSS A GORILLA AND A SNAKE? A. KING LONG!

HA HA

# Hide and Sneak

Camouflage is the way that many animals are shaped and colored to blend into the scenery around them. It comes in handy when there are hungry hunters everywhere, ready to gobble them up. But camouflage also helps the hunters sneak up on their prey.

**EXTRA! EXTRA!**
The katydid gets its name from the noise a male makes to attract a female — "katy-did, katy-didn't!"

**Q. WHAT DO YOU CALL A STICK INSECT WITH A COLD?**

**A. A sick insect!**

HA HA

Sneaking around the Amazon rain forest is this insect called a leaf katydid. It's disguised as a leaf so it can't be spotted. Even the veins on its wings look exactly like the veins on a leaf.

# Shady Baby

For extra protection from hungry animals, a baby tapir is colored differently from its black-and-white parents. It has splotchy stripes and spots running down its body that make it hard to see among the shadows on the shady forest floor.

# Lucky Stripe

The brown and white stripes on the African okapi make it hard to spot among the trees, while it munches on leaves. Its stripes make it look as if it is related to the zebra, but it's really a distant cousin of the giraffe!

# Spot the Spots!

The leopard's spots help it to blend into a leafy background. It hunts animals in Africa, such as small antelope. It waits until its prey, or victim, is very near. Then it pounces!

## That's Weird!

Stick insects not only look like twigs, but they act like twigs, too. They sway gently in the breeze, just like the plants they live among. They're really hard to spot!

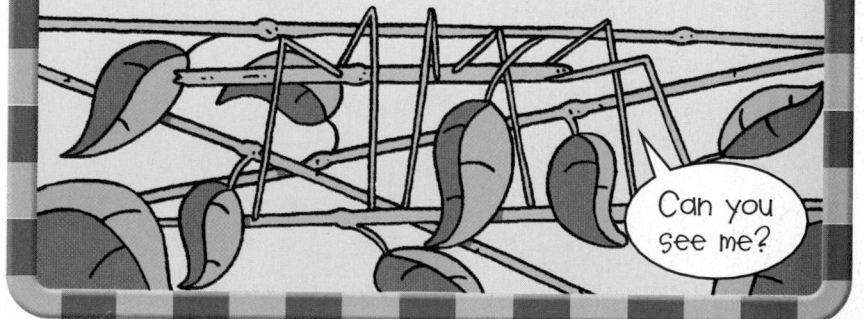

# Color crazy!

Many animals in the rain forest are anything but camouflaged. Instead they stand out, loud and clear, with bright colors. There is usually a reason why animals look and act the way they do. In the rain forest, looking flashy is all about survival.

## Dangerous Beauty

The coral snake may look pretty, but its red, black, and yellow stripes are a warning sign to attackers — this snake is poisonous! When frightened, the coral snake protects itself by curling up its body, tucking in its head, and sticking its tail in the air instead.

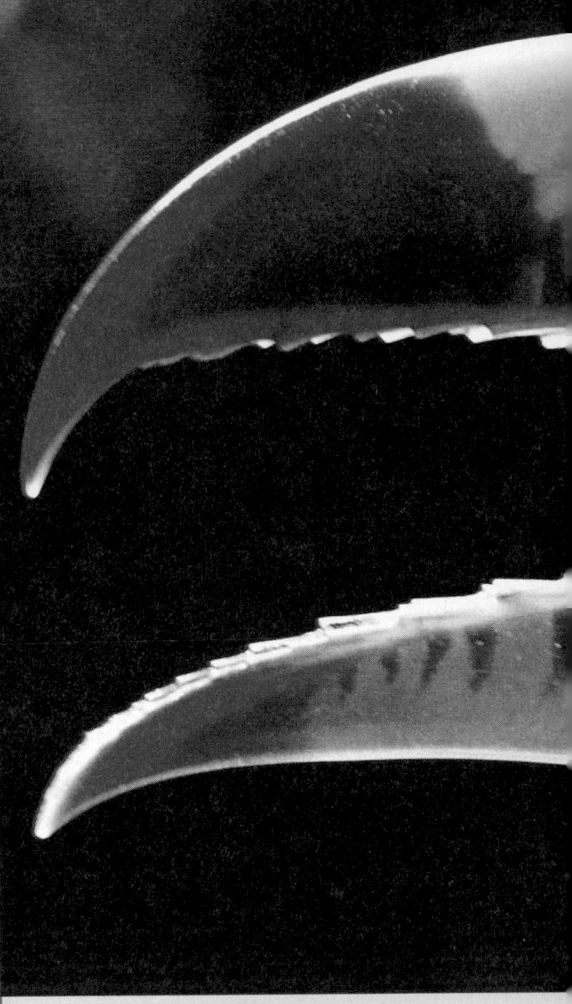

## Tall Squawker

Parrots come in a whole range of colors, like crayons in a box. This helps them to recognize one another. There are many types of parrots, such as macaws, cockatoos, and parakeets. The largest is the hyacinth macaw, which grows as tall as a four-year-old child!

**EXTRA! EXTRA!** Each toucan's beak has a slightly different color and pattern. It is made of keratin — the same material as your fingernails!

▲ This bird is hard to miss! The toucan uses its beak like a saw to eat fruit. It may also use it to attract mates and scare enemies. The beak is hollow, so it's not as heavy as it looks.

# Bad Taste

The passionflower butterfly has a bitter taste. Animals brave enough to eat it remember the experience and don't try it again. There are nicer-tasting butterflies that copy its bright markings to scare enemies away, too!

You taste horrible!

# That's Weird!

Poison arrow frogs make some of the world's deadliest poisons in their skin. As a warning to attackers, the frogs come in a range of bright colors from radiant red to blooming blue!

HA HA

17

# creepy crawly World!

The rain forest is teeming with beetles, spiders, scorpions, ants, and all their creepy crawly cousins. These creatures do many important jobs that keep the rain forest alive, such as providing food for other animals and spreading pollen for the plant life.

The tarantula's poison is not very strong. It uses it to paralyze its prey, such as this insect, rather than to kill it. A fluid turns the prey into pulp for the spider to suck up. Slurp!

# Say your Prayers

The female praying mantis strikes a pose like a person saying her prayers. But she's really waiting for an insect to fly by. Then she becomes a "preying" praying mantis! She claps her prey between her waiting legs and gobbles it up in seconds!

# Leaves on Parade

One of the strangest sights in the rain forest is a long, long parade of leaves marching across the forest floor. Take a closer look and you'll see leaf-cutter ants carrying leaf pieces they've cut with their sharp mouths. They chew up the leaves to make them soft, then eat the fungus that grows on the leaves.

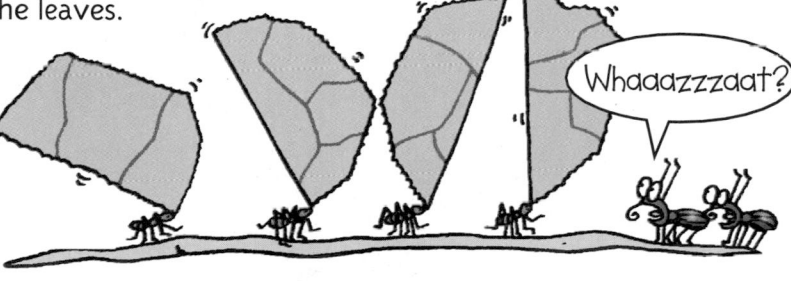

Whaaazzzaat?

## Wow!

A millipede eats dead leaves and branches and helps turn old trees back into rich soil. The name *millipede* means "a thousand legs," but these animals only have up to 330 legs. When a millipede is threatened, it shoots out stinky juices from its body to make enemies leave it alone.

# Who is dressed the best?

You want me to lift THAT?

The male rhinoceros beetle has a horn on its head, which it uses to lift objects more than 850 times its own weight. That's like you lifting five small cars!

Eek!

The female black widow spider has a red hourglass shape on her body. But don't look too closely or your time will be up!

Gorgeous, but deadly!

One rare beetle is colored gold! But underneath this shiny coat hides a real terror. It chomps through trees and destroys them at an alarming rate!

# Strange Neighbors

Each rain forest animal is surrounded by a collection of bizarre neighbors. But strangeness isn't just an oddity — it may help in the daily struggle for survival. Here are a few animals with unusual ways of staying alive!

## Running Bird

The Australian cassowary would make a meaty meal for any hunter. The trick is catching it. Even though this bird can't fly, it can run away at speeds of 30 mph (48 kmh) — as fast as a cyclist on a racing bike. If you do corner one, watch out. It has a bladelike claw on each foot!

**EXTRA! EXTRA!**
The chameleon changes color to hide from an attacker. If that fails, it plays dead until the enemy goes away!

## Wow!

The Cuban bee hummingbird is the smallest bird in the world. It is only 1 inch (2.5 cm) long, about as big as a bee. It weighs less than a piece of paper and its eggs are smaller than jellybeans. This tiny bird zigzags through the air to avoid ending up as somebody's lunch.

Ha! You missed!

# Supersquirrel!

The flying squirrel can escape from trouble even when it's trapped up a tree. It just spreads out its legs and leaps. The extra skin between its legs becomes glider wings, allowing the squirrel to sail through the air safely to the next tree.

The chameleon's strange eyes move in opposite directions, scanning for passing insects. When an insect comes along, the chameleon's long, sticky tongue shoots out and grabs it!

# Night Life!

You might think the rain forest is quiet at night, but you'd be wrong. Animals on the night shift wake up and start looking for breakfast. So if you want to see some interesting feeding habits, nighttime is the right time to do it!

## Scared Stiff

The opossum has tiny eyes and can barely see a thing at night. It makes up for its lack of eyesight with sharp senses of hearing and smell. When frightened, one type of opossum falls into a state of shock and appears dead!

The black flying fox is really a bat! At night, it flies off on huge wings to find a meal of fruit.

# Blood Bat

**1** The vampire bat of South America spends its days hanging upside down in caves. Here, it sleeps, grooms itself, and chats with other bats.

*Hey, going out tonight?*

**2** The bat uses a clever trick to find its way in the dark. It sends out sounds and listens for them to bounce back off things.

**3** When the bat finds its favorite food, such as a cow, it bites. A chemical in the bat's spit stops the victim's wound from healing. Then the bat slurps up the blood!

*zzzzz*

## Ball of Armor

The armadillo is covered in tough plates that are made from hairs stuck together. It wanders around at night sniffing for insects on the forest floor. If it's scared, it simply rolls into a tight, armored ball to protect its soft underbelly.

*It's OK, it's only me!*

## That's Weird!

The aye-aye lives in Madagascar, a large island off the coast of Africa. To find food, it taps on a tree with its incredibly long finger. It can tell by the sound if there is an insect grub inside. Now the big finger comes into use again, as the aye-aye digs out the tasty treat!

*Anybody home?*

## Jeepers Peepers

The African bush baby uses its huge eyes to help it find insects in the dark. At night, the middles of its eyes, called the pupils, become superwide. This helps it to see in the small amount of moonlight that cuts through the thick canopy.

# Killer cats!

The big cats are the most fearsome creatures in the rain forest. They are predators — animals that hunt other animals for food. They prowl the forest floor or climb into the branches to grab their prey. Most cats are camouflaged so that they can sneak up on their victims.

▲ The jaguar is the biggest and fiercest cat in the Amazon. It usually preys on large animals, such as the peccary. Jaguars live alone and sometimes get mean if another jaguar comes too close!

# Meat Feast

The tiger lives in Asia, where it sleeps all day and hunts all night. When it finds a buffalo or other meaty beast, the tiger spears it with its sharp claws and then sinks its teeth into its victim's neck. It often hides the meat somewhere where other meat eaters can't find it. The tiger then returns to feed off it for several days.

Now where did I leave your dinner?

## EXTRA! EXTRA!

The jaguar has even more powerful jaws than other big cats. It can crunch through a river turtle's shell in one bite!

# Nice Neighbors

Ocelots are wildcats that live in the Amazon, along with jaguars. The ocelot is smaller than the jaguar and would much rather eat a monkey or a snake than a big deer. The two kinds of cats eat different kinds of food, so they live alongside each other in peace.

# That's Weird!

The black panther is exactly the same species, or type of animal, as the spotted leopard. The only difference is that it has a black coat. Most black panthers have at least one spotted parent and lots of spotted brothers and sisters.

# Forest Future

Rain forests have existed for millions of years and are vital to the earth's future. Half of the world's species of plants and animals live here and the trees produce oxygen for us to breathe. But nowadays, the rain forests are shrinking — fast!

## Forest Families

In rain forests around the world, different tribes, or groups, of people live in small communities. They hunt animals and gather plants to feed themselves and to trade with others. The people take only what they need from the rain forest and live in harmony with it.

## Under Threat

Today, rain forests are vanishing fast. Land is being cleared of trees to make farmland and to dig mines for minerals, such as copper and iron. Trees are chopped down for wood and for making paper. As a result, the animals, plants, and traditional tribes of the rain forests are in danger.

## Wow!

Every year, enough rain forest is destroyed to fill the whole state of Texas. So far, over half of the world's rain forests have been cut down. And the bad news is that the speed of destruction is getting faster. At this rate, the forests will all be gone by the year 2030!

TEXAS

## Should we save the rain forests?

People live here! If the rain forests are destroyed, the tribes will lose their homes. Their knowledge of life in the rain forests will be lost to us forever.

Millions of different kinds of animals and plants live here, too. Creatures, such as the blue morpho butterfly, are under threat because their homes are disappearing.

Scientists discover new food and medicines that can be harvested from rain forest plants. The rain forests have to be protected for our future!

These Piaroa Indians, from the Amazon rain forest in Venezuela, are on a hunting trip.

# Extra Amazing

The rain forest is a land of record breakers. So journey deep into the forest and check out some of the largest, loudest, smelliest, and oddest animals on Earth.

## Loud Mouth

Howler monkeys of Central and South America earn their name every time they let out their deafening cry. The howler monkey is one of the noisiest animals in the world. To enable him to shout loudly, the male has an extra-large voice box. His roar can be heard up to 2 miles (3 km) away!

## Slothfully Slow

The three-toed sloth is the slowest mammal on Earth. It travels fastest when it's in the trees, but even then it's so unbearably slow that you can hardly see it moving. Tiny plants called algae grow on its fur and turn it green, so only the sharpest predators notice it among the thick rain forest leaves. It spends its whole life hanging upside down in the trees, except for once-a-week trips to the ground.

Go slow!

## Stickiest Stinker

The South American tamandua, an anteater, makes an unbearable stench that has earned it the nickname "stinker of the forest." It also has some of the stickiest spit in the world. It pokes a gooey tongue or spit-soaked finger into a tree and pulls out hundreds of crunchy critters

Ugh!

## Eagle Eyes

The harpy eagle is the largest eagle in the world. It lives in the Amazon rain forest and is very rare. Its wingspan is 7 feet (2 m) — as wide as a basketball player is tall! The harpy eagle's sharp eyesight helps it to spot prey. It can even see a sloth creeping through the trees. It is so powerful that it can pull its prey from the branches even when its victim is hanging on tight.

## Giant Creepy Crawly

The goliath beetle is the biggest bug in the world. It grows up to 4.5 inches (11.5 cm) long — big enough to fill the palm of your hand. It likes to eat dead plants and dung. That may sound pretty smelly, but the goliath beetle does a really good job of cleaning up after other rain forest dwellers!

## Major Snake!

A contender for the world's biggest snake is the South American anaconda. It's not the world's longest snake, but it's probably the heaviest. The largest anaconda ever measured wasn't weighed, but it was 44 inches (112 cm) around its middle — the same as a grown man. It probably weighed nearly 500 pounds (227 kg).

# True or False?

**How much do you really know about the rain forest? Test yourself and say whether each of these statements is true or false. Answers are on page 32, but no cheating!**

1. There are lots of rain forests across North America.

2. The understory is the greenest layer of the rain forest.

3. The harpy eagle is the largest eagle on Earth.

4. The flying pig lives in the rain forest.

5. The pitcher plant traps bugs and then eats them.

6. An orangutan's arms are long enough to reach its ankles.

7. This flower smells like rotting meat.

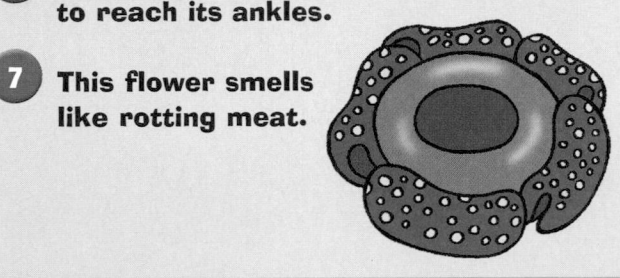

# Rain Forest Terms

**camouflage**
Colors and markings that help an animal to blend in with its surroundings so that it can't be seen.

**canopy**
A thick layer of branches and leaves in the treetops, between the emergent layer and the mid-canopy.

**emergent layer**
Trees that are taller than the surrounding ones.

**equator**
An imaginary line drawn around the middle of the earth.

**insect**
An animal without a backbone that has a three-part body, two feelers called antennae, and six legs.

**mammal**
An animal that breathes air, has body hair, and gives birth to babies that feed on mother's milk. Monkeys, cats, rats, and humans are all mammals.

**mid-canopy**
Small trees and bushes that grow in the rain forest, between the canopy and the forest floor, or understory.

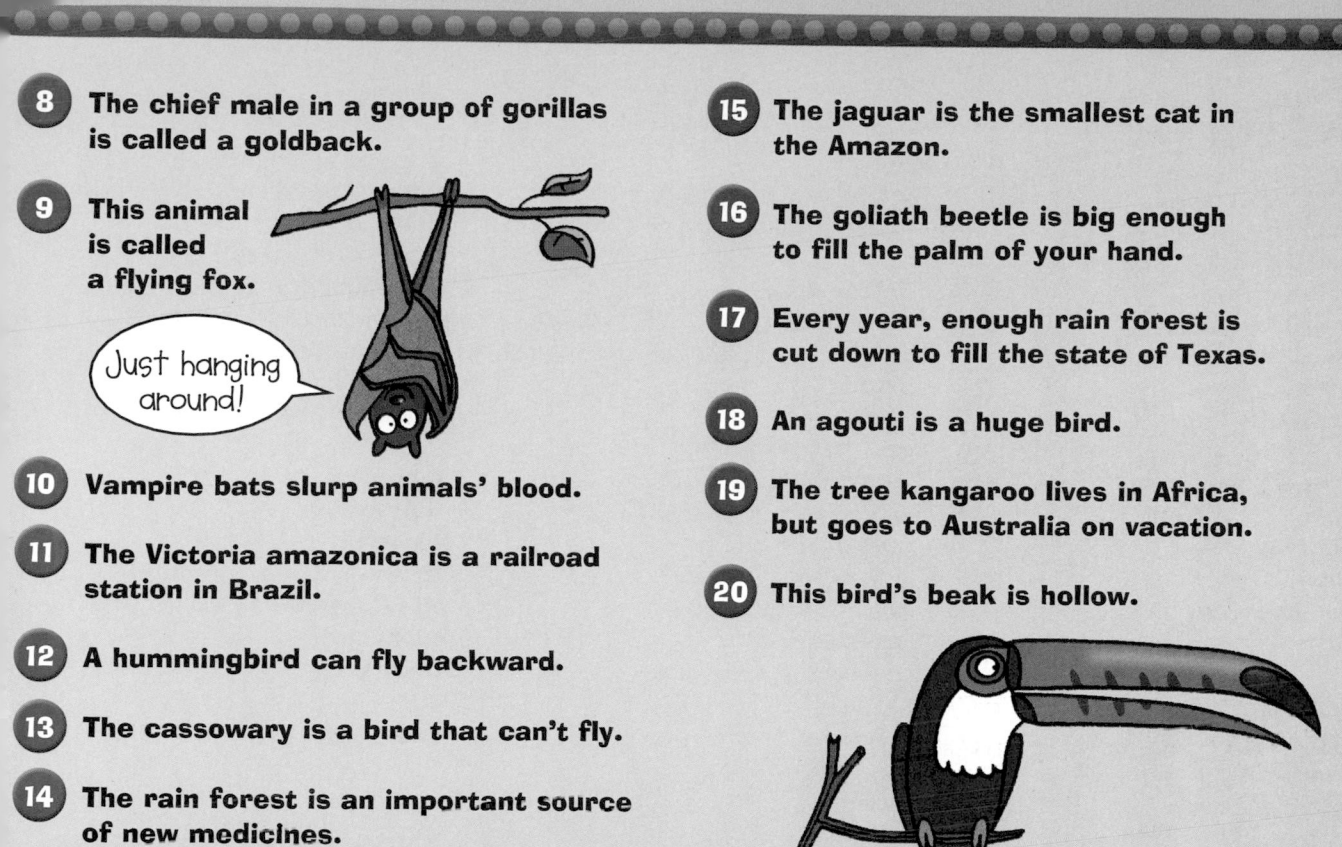

**8** The chief male in a group of gorillas is called a goldback.

**9** This animal is called a flying fox.

*Just hanging around!*

**10** Vampire bats slurp animals' blood.

**11** The Victoria amazonica is a railroad station in Brazil.

**12** A hummingbird can fly backward.

**13** The cassowary is a bird that can't fly.

**14** The rain forest is an important source of new medicines.

**15** The jaguar is the smallest cat in the Amazon.

**16** The goliath beetle is big enough to fill the palm of your hand.

**17** Every year, enough rain forest is cut down to fill the state of Texas.

**18** An agouti is a huge bird.

**19** The tree kangaroo lives in Africa, but goes to Australia on vacation.

**20** This bird's beak is hollow.

**nectar**
A sugary substance that is made by flowers. Many birds and insects feed on nectar. The plant uses nectar to attract animals in order to spread pollen to other plants.

**pollen**
A yellow dust made by flowering plants. Pollen contains male cells that are carried to female cells by animals, wind or water, in order for new plants to grow. This is called pollination.

**predator**
An animal that hunts, kills, and eats other animals.

**prey**
An animal that is hunted and eaten by other animals.

**rain forest**
A forest that grows in hot, wet parts of the world, near the equator. Rain forests are packed with an enormous variety of animal and plant life.

**tropics**
A warm area found between two imaginary lines circling the earth. They are called the tropic of Cancer, which is north of the equator, and the tropic of Capricorn, which is south of the equator.

**understory**
The lowest level of the rain forest. This is an extremely dark, damp place. Many seeds grow into young plants here.

**vine**
A woody, climbing plant.

# Index

## Answers

| | | | |
|---|---|---|---|
| 1 | False | 11 | False |
| 2 | False | 12 | True |
| 3 | True | 13 | True |
| 4 | False | 14 | True |
| 5 | True | 15 | False |
| 6 | True | 16 | True |
| 7 | True | 17 | True |
| 8 | False | 18 | False |
| 9 | True | 19 | False |
| 10 | True | 20 | True |

**Author:** Paul Dawson
**Illustrations:** Andrew Peters
**Consultant:** Barbara Taylor BSc.
**Photographs:** Cover: orangutan OSF/Konrad Rothe; p. 3 FLPA/Minden Pictures/F. Lanting; p. 4 NHPA/Andy Rouse; p. 6 SPL/Art Wolfe; p. 7 NHPA/Stephen Dalton; p. 9 OSF/Richard Packwood; p. 10 Bruce Coleman/Alain Compost; p. 11 Corbis/Purcell Team; p. 13 OSF/Daniel J. Fox; p. 14 Michael and Patricia Fogden; p. 15 NHPA/Martin Wendler; p. 16 OSF/ Michael Fogden; pp. 16–17 Michael and Patricia Fogden; p. 18 Michael and Patricia Fogden; p. 21 top OSF/Photo Researchers/Nick Bergkessel; pp. 20–21 bottom NHPA Norbert Wu; p. 22 Ardea/Hans and Judy Beste; p. 23 Corbis/Gallo Images; pp. 24–25 Bruce Coleman/Luiz Claudio Marigo; p. 25 Ardea/Adrian Warren; p. 27 Ardea/Nick Gordon; p. 29 Corbis/Kevin Schafer.

ISBN 0-439-28601-8

12 11 10 9 8 7 6 5 4 3          3 4 5 6/0

Printed in the U.S.A.

First Scholastic printing, November 2001